TIME-OUT TRIVIA FOR MARCH

An Activity for Every Day

Written by Becky Daniel

Illustrated by Nancee McClure

Cover by Nancee McClure

Copyright © 1994, Good Apple

Good Apple
1204 Buchanan St., Box 299
Carthage, IL 62321-0299

Paramount Publishing

Copyright © 1994, Good Apple

ISBN No. 0-86653-786-4

Printing No. 98765432

Good Apple
1204 Buchanan St., Box 299
Carthage, IL 62321-0299

Table of Contents

GA1480

To the Teacher

Each daily fact in this series of trivia books is based on historical and modern events designed to delight and motivate students, and help them make important, human connections with people who lived and accomplished interesting things many years ago or who still live and make a difference in our world today. People from other places will come alive for your students when they eagerly bite off another bit of daily trivia. For children who choose to take their learning a step further, a bonus activity is included on each page.

Special March events include International Women's Day, Buzzards' Day, National Goof-Off Day, National Pig Day, Saint Patrick's Day, and many others. Activities include paper airplanes, origami, a magic number trick, poetry writing, solving codes, planning a meal, and much, much more.

You will know the very best way to present these activities in your classroom. But whether you use them as lesson extenders, in learning centers, or as daily sponge activities, children are certain to enjoy these engaging activities as they learn more about history. For your convenience, a reproducible weather trivia calendar and award certificates are also included with this set of fun and educational trivia-based work sheets.

Hooray for American Red Cross

It's American Red Cross Month. One function of the Red Cross is to offer first aid to people. Do you own a first aid kit? What are some things that you might find in a first aid kit? Put a check by each thing that you feel is important to include in a first aid kit.

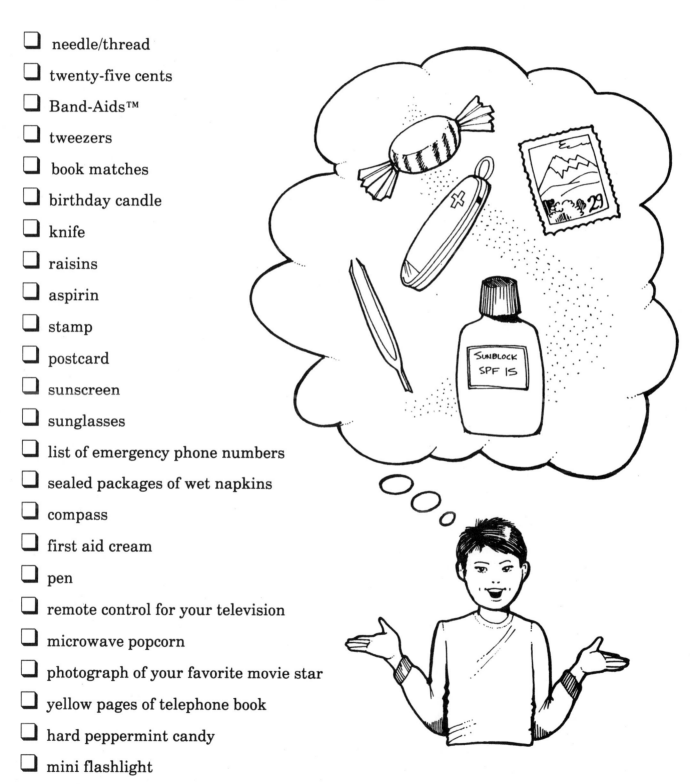

- ❑ needle/thread
- ❑ twenty-five cents
- ❑ Band-Aids™
- ❑ tweezers
- ❑ book matches
- ❑ birthday candle
- ❑ knife
- ❑ raisins
- ❑ aspirin
- ❑ stamp
- ❑ postcard
- ❑ sunscreen
- ❑ sunglasses
- ❑ list of emergency phone numbers
- ❑ sealed packages of wet napkins
- ❑ compass
- ❑ first aid cream
- ❑ pen
- ❑ remote control for your television
- ❑ microwave popcorn
- ❑ photograph of your favorite movie star
- ❑ yellow pages of telephone book
- ❑ hard peppermint candy
- ❑ mini flashlight

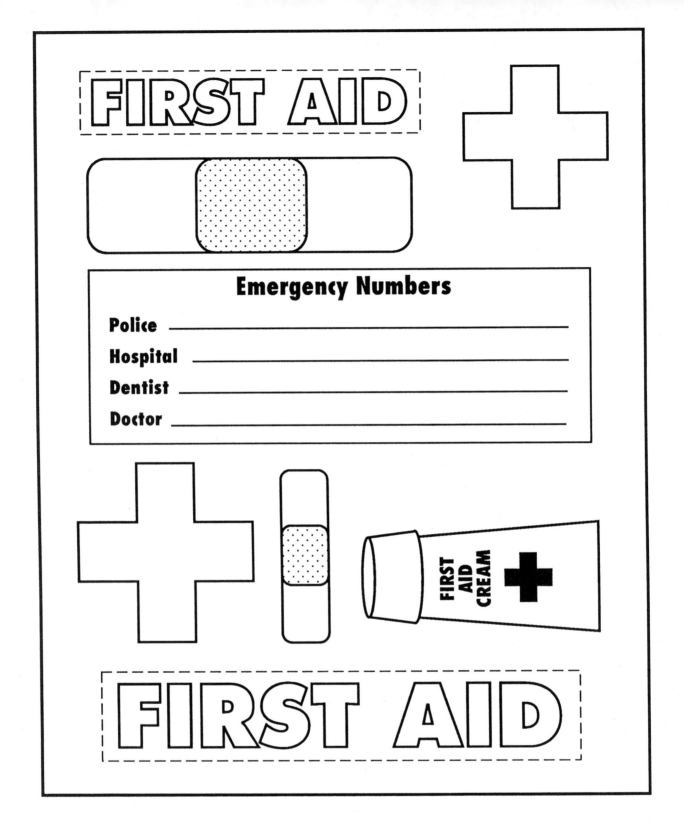

FIRST AID

Emergency Numbers

Police _____

Hospital _____

Dentist _____

Doctor _____

FIRST AID CREAM

FIRST AID

Bonus: *Design and assemble a first aid kit. Cut out some of the designs above, color them and glue them onto a small box. (Girl Scouts often make tiny portable first aid kits using metal Band-Aid™ boxes.) Put in some of the items you have checked on the first aid list. Take your first aid kit with you when you go on long bike rides, hiking, camping, and overnight visits to a friend's house.*

GA1480

National Pig Day!

Today is National Pig Day! Did you know that pigs are one of the most intelligent animals? Celebrate pigs today with this "piggy" assignment. Do you know how to read, write, or speak in pig Latin? (Pig Latin is a coded version of English. You simply put the initial letter of a word at the end of the word and add the letters *ay* afterwards. Example: oybay = boy, atcay = cat.) See if you can decode the question below.

Fiay hetay igbay, adbay olfway oldtay hetay torysay foay hetay hreetay ittlelay igspay, hatway ouldway tiay ebay ikelay?

_____

_____

_____

_____

_____

Bonus: *In pig Latin, write your answer to the question you decoded.*

GA1480

Happy Birthday, Texas

On this day in 1836, Texas issued its Declaration of Independence from Mexico. If you could declare your independence from something, what would it be? Use the Declaration of Independence certificate below to let the world know from what you would like to be free.

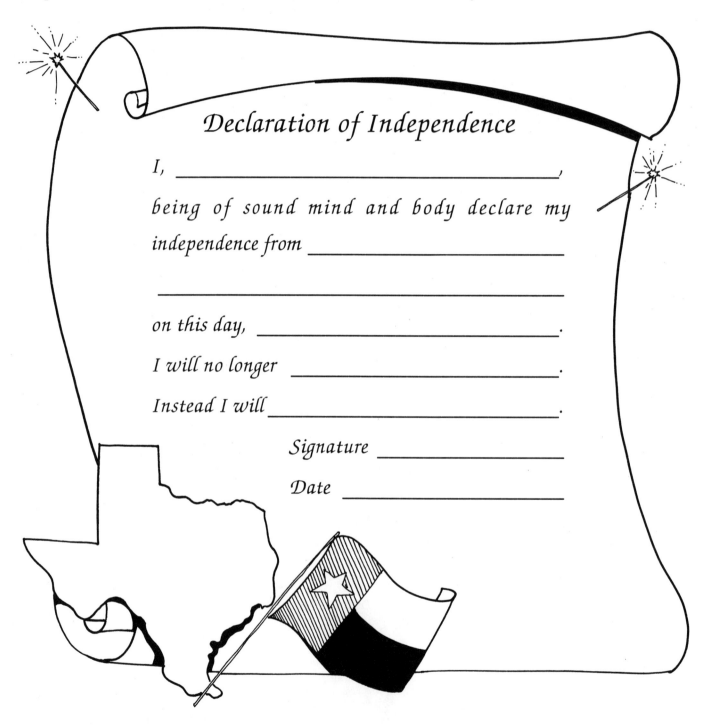

Declaration of Independence

I, _____,

being of sound mind and body declare my

independence from _____

_____

on this day, _____.

I will no longer _____.

Instead I will _____.

Signature _____

Date _____

Bonus: *Cut out your declaration and attach it to a sheet of black construction paper. Hang it in your room.*

4

Happy Hinamatsuri

Hinamatsuri is a special doll festival for girls that takes place throughout Japan on this day. Celebrate Hinamatsuri by creating some paper dolls for a little person you know. Before you begin, you may want to mount the doll patterns and clothes on construction paper. Cut out dolls and clothes. Color the clothes. Make additional clothes to fit the dolls.

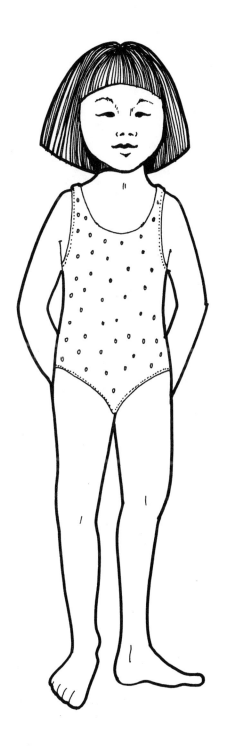
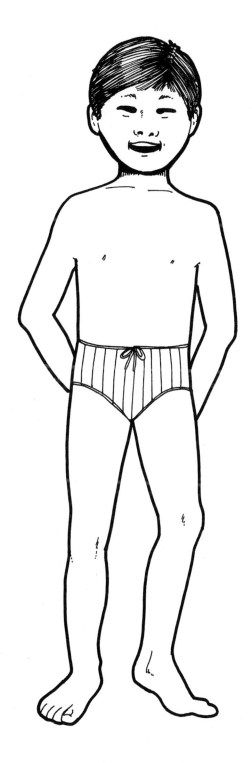

GA1480

Bonus: *When you finish making the dolls, present them to a little friend. Tell the person about Hinamatsuri.*

6

GA1480

Happy Birthday, Jane Goodall

Jane Goodall, an anthropologist, was born on March 4, 1934. Jane loved animals and did extensive research on apes. She learned how to care for them. Do you have a pet? Pretend you have lost a pet. Write a short newspaper advertisement and design a sign showing what your pet looks like, where it was lost, and how you can be reached.

Lost and Found

NOTICE

Bonus: *Pretend your lost pet was returned to you by a small child. Write a thank-you note to the child expressing your gratitude.*

GA1480

Boston Massacre

On this day in 1770, British troops and a crowd of citizens in Boston got into a fight. Five men were killed and six others were injured by British troops. This confrontation contributed to the already unpopular situation of the British troops in America. Some think that this event contributed to the beginning of the American Revolution. Use the five tombstones below to write epitaphs honoring the five men who were killed at the Boston Massacre.

Bonus: *Use an encyclopedia or other reference books to learn more about the Boston Massacre.*

8

Happy Birthday, Mike!

This is the birthday of the famous artist, Michelangelo, born in Italy on March 6, 1475. Some of his well-known works include the sculpture entitled *David* and the painting on the ceiling of the Sistine Chapel. On the palette below, use paints to create a happy birthday salute to Michelangelo.

Bonus: *Write a two-line, rhyming salute for your card.*

Texas Cowboy Poetry Gathering

At about this time each year in Alpine, Texas, cowboys gather for poetry readings. Many country western songs and poems are about the cowboys' dogs or horses. Write a short cowboy poem.

Bonus: *Read your poem to at least five different friends.*

10

GA1480

National PTA Drug and Alcohol Awareness Week

Each year the National PTA sponsors an alcohol and drug awareness week. Schools participate in a number of different ways. In the box found below, design a poster that warns youngsters about the dangers of drugs or alcohol. Your poster should include a catchy slogan.

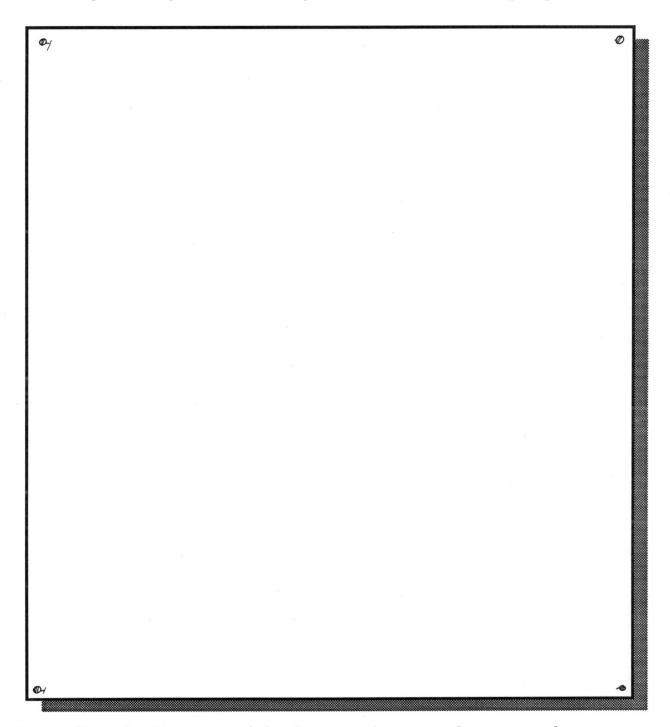

Bonus: *Use a familiar tune and the slogan you have created to create a drug awareness jingle. Sing your jingle to three children younger than yourself.*

International Women's Day

Today is a day to honor women. In celebration of a woman you admire, complete the poster on page 13. After you have completed it, cut out both pages and mount them on construction paper or light cardboard. Share with the woman you most admire.

The name of a woman I admire is _____.
Here's a picture I drew of her.

Here are three facts about her life. 1. _____

                          2. _____

                          3. _____

I admire her because _____.

Here is a poem I wrote about her.

_____

_____

_____

_____

_____

_____

An Admirable Woman

Name _____

Dog in Space

The first dog to travel in space was launched in *Sputnik 9* on this day in 1961. To celebrate the first dog in space, decorate and color the paper airplane below. Then cut on the solid lines and fold on the dotted lines.

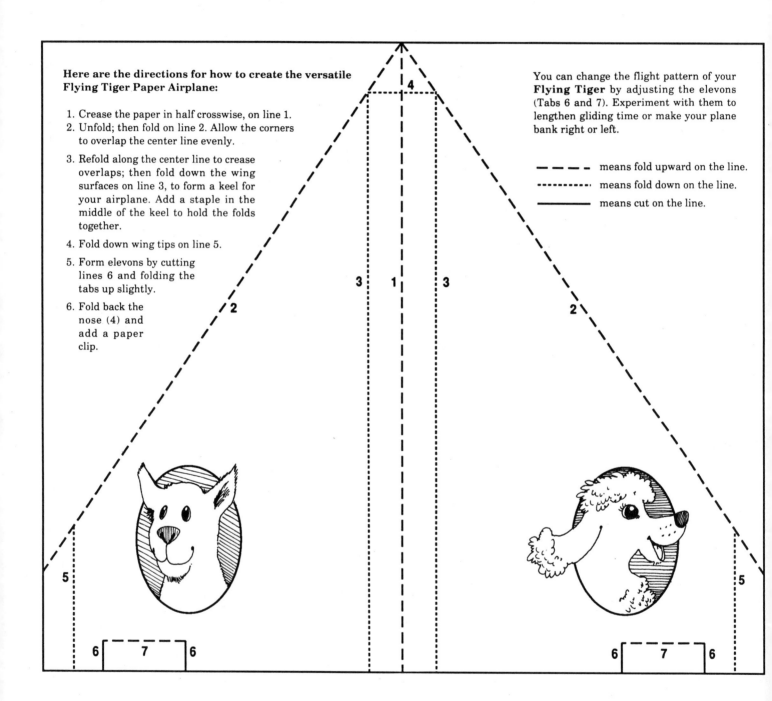

Here are the directions for how to create the versatile Flying Tiger Paper Airplane:

1. Crease the paper in half crosswise, on line 1.
2. Unfold; then fold on line 2. Allow the corners to overlap the center line evenly.

3. Refold along the center line to crease overlaps; then fold down the wing surfaces on line 3, to form a keel for your airplane. Add a staple in the middle of the keel to hold the folds together.

4. Fold down wing tips on line 5.

5. Form elevons by cutting lines 6 and folding the tabs up slightly.

6. Fold back the nose (4) and add a paper clip.

You can change the flight pattern of your **Flying Tiger** by adjusting the elevons (Tabs 6 and 7). Experiment with them to lengthen gliding time or make your plane bank right or left.

— — — — means fold upward on the line.

··········· means fold down on the line.

————— means cut on the line.

Bonus: *See if your plane will fly straight, stall, loop, bank right, and bank left. Complete the test flight record sheet on the next page.*

14

GA1480

Paper Airplane
Test Flight Record Sheet

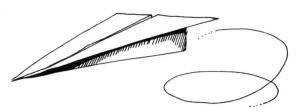

Flight	1	2	3	4	5	6	7	8	9	10
Straight?										
Stalled?										
Looped?										
Banked?										
Distance										

Comments

Flight 1 _____

_____

Flight 2 _____

_____

Flight 3 _____

_____

Flight 4 _____

_____

Flight 5 _____

_____

Flight 6 _____

_____

Flight 7 _____

_____

Flight 8 _____

_____

Flight 9 _____

_____

Flight 10 _____

_____

GA1480

Ring! Ring! Ringgggggg!

The telephone was invented by Alexander Graham Bell on March 10, 1876. Do you ever wonder what the first telephone number was? Use the letter-number code on the telephone below to think of clever telephone numbers for each occupation listed below. To get you started, several have been done for you.

1	ABC 2	DEF 3
GHI 4	JKL 5	MNO 6
PRS 7	TUV 8	WXY 9
*	0	#

barber shop	288-4247	cut-hair
preschool	386-4543	fun-4kid
doctor	_____	_____
dentist	_____	_____
lawyer	_____	_____
songwriter	_____	_____
manicurist	_____	_____
house painter	_____	_____
teacher	_____	_____
zookeeper	_____	_____
accountant	_____	_____

Bonus: *Make up a good telephone number that people might associate with you.*

16

GA1480

March 11
Human Services Day

Today is the day set aside to recognize and honor people involved in the social work profession. Why do you think some people dedicate their lives to helping other people? Do you know someone who spends a great deal of time working to help others? Use the award certificate below to recognize that person.

Award Certificate

We appreciate

you, _____,

because you _____

_____

_____

_____.

Presented this day, _____

19 _____

_____

Signature

Bonus: *Cut out the certificate. Present your award certificate to the person you want to honor.*

Girl Scouts

Juliet Low founded the Girl Scouts of America on this day in 1912. Today there are millions of Girl Scouts in America. One of the projects that most Girl Scouts work on is badge attainment. Girl Scouts can earn badges in health, world of people, arts, out-of-doors, and many other areas. The design on each badge shows what the activity was about. Design a new Girl Scout badge in the circle, and on the lines at the bottom of the page, list five things the Girl Scout must do to earn the badge.

1. _____

2. _____

3. _____

4. _____

5. _____

Bonus: *Make up a name for the badge you created.*

18

GA1480

New Planets Discovered

On March 13, 1781, the planet Uranus was discovered. Nearly fifty years later, in 1830, the announcement of the discovery of Pluto was made on this same date. Pretend you have been selected to put a note in a space capsule that will be launched to Pluto. Remember, the English language will not have meaning to someone living in outer space. What message will you try to communicate, and how will you present the message so it will be understood?

Bonus: *Test your ability to communicate. Give your message to an adult and see if he or she can tell you the meaning of the message.*

Storytelling Weekend

Professional storytellers gather to conduct workshops, critique storytellers, and tell stories on a weekend in March each year in Greenup, Kentucky. What do you think makes a good storyteller? Make a list of ten things.

Good Storytelling Musts!

1. _____
2. _____
3. _____
4. _____
5. _____
6. _____
7. _____
8. _____
9. _____
10. _____

Bonus: *Tell a story to a little child. Remember to do all of the things you put on your Good Storytelling list.*

Rock "Ramblin' Rob"!

On March 14, 1986, "Ramblin' Rob" McDonald sat down in a rocking chair in the window of the Pizza Factory in Mariposa, California, and started rocking. He didn't stop rocking until April 2. Altogether he rocked 453 hours and 40 minutes. Do you wonder how "Ramblin' Rob" looked after all that rocking? Draw a picture of how you think he might have looked after rocking more than eighteen days in the chair below.

Bonus: *If you could spend days and days doing the same thing over and over, what would it be? Write a paragraph about your idea of a record-setting event in which you would like to participate.*

21

Buzzards' Day

Each year on this day, the buzzards return to Hinckley, Ohio, from their winter home in the Great Smoky Mountains. To make a reminder of this interesting bird phenomenon, enlarge, cut, and fold the pattern below to create an origami buzzard.

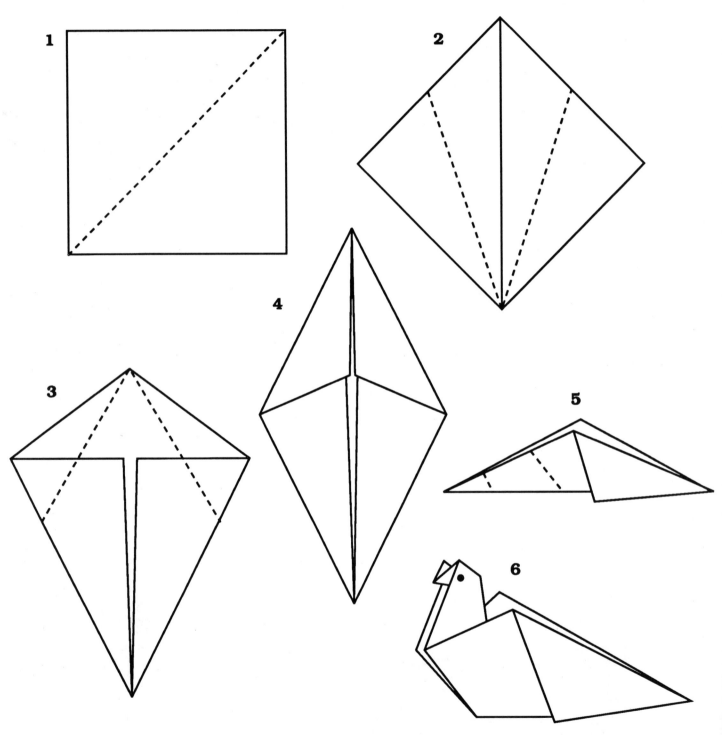

Bonus: *Find out how to make other origami animals. Teach your new skill to a friend.*

March 16

An Expensive Stamp!

On this day in 1985 in Germany, a stamp was sold at an auction for $864,386. The stamp was first issued in 1851. It was accidentally printed on blue-green paper instead of dull rose. Do you wonder what the stamp looked like? If you were asked to design a stamp, what would it look like? Use the stamp below to show your design.

Bonus: *How many regular postage stamps could be bought with the amount paid for the one sold at the auction in Germany on March 16, 1985?*

Happy St. Patrick's Day

Today is St. Patrick's Day! This is the day the Irish set aside to commemorate the patron saint of Ireland, Bishop Patrick. Green is the traditional color used to celebrate St. Patrick's Day. Pretend you are having an Irish party and plan to serve all green foods. Draw a picture and label the foods you plan to serve.

Bonus: *Write the recipe for creating a green party dessert or punch.*

Happy Birthday, Mr. President

The twenty-second and twenty-fourth President of the United States was born on this day in 1837. He was the only President to be married in the White House, and his daughter was the first child of a President to be born in the White House. To discover the face of the mystery President, cut apart the puzzle pieces below. After putting the puzzle together correctly, glue the pieces in the correct order on another sheet of paper.

GROVER CLEVELAND

22nd President of the United States, 1885-1889

24th President of the United States, 1893-1897

Born: March 18, 1837 in Caldwell, New Jersey

Died: June 24, 1908, in Princeton, New Jersey

Bonus: *Find five additional facts about this President. Write them on the back of your assembled puzzle.*

Return of the Swallows

Today is the day the swallows usually return to San Juan Capistrano. To celebrate the return of the swallows, use the nine frames in the filmstrip below to illustrate a story of a swallow returning to the old California mission.

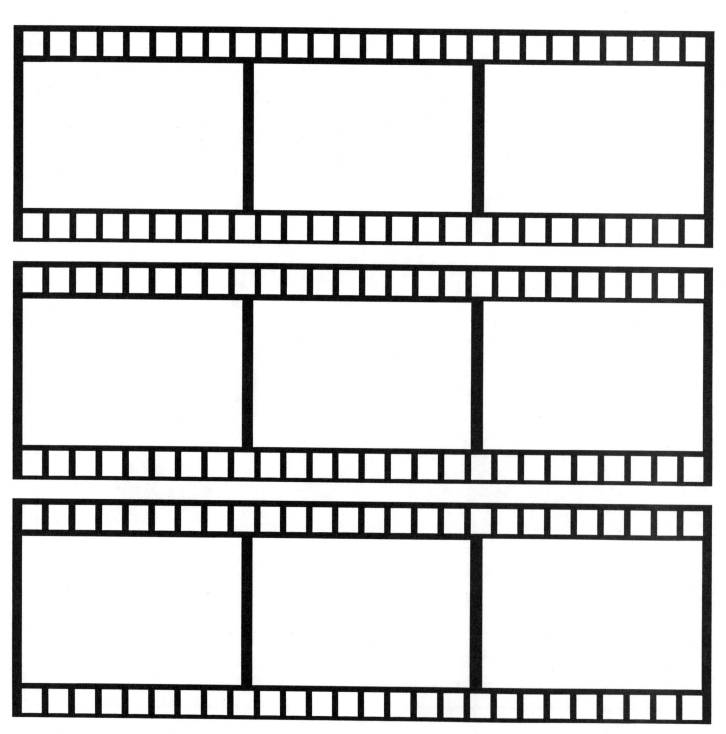

Bonus: *Write narration for your nine frames on the filmstrip.*

26

GA1480

March 20

Happy Birthday, Fred and Bird

This is the birthday of two of children's television favorites, Mr. Rogers and Big Bird. If Big Bird and Mr. Rogers had a birthday lunch, what do you think they would discuss? Write the conversation that you think they might have in the bubbles.

Bonus: *If you had lunch with Mr. Rogers and Big Bird, what would you like to ask each one? Write your questions. Then write the answers you think each would give.*

27

GA1480

Johann Sebastian Bach

Johann Sebastian Bach was born on this day in 1685. Today, three hundred years later, people are still enjoying the work of this musical genius. In honor of this great musician, use the letters in the musical scale to spell as many words as you can. Example: face. You may repeat letters in a word. Example: egg

1. _____

2. _____

3. _____

4. _____

5. _____

6. _____

7. _____

8. _____

9. _____

10. _____

11. _____

12. _____

13. _____

14. _____

15. _____

16. _____

17. _____

18. _____

19. _____

20. _____

21. _____

22. _____

23. _____

24. _____

Bonus: *Can you write a sentence using only the letters found on the musical scale?*

National Goof-Off Day

March 22 has been declared a day of relaxation. Take time to enjoy life. People deserve to enjoy and relax. Sometimes adults get caught up in their work and forget to play like children. Use the invitation below to invite an adult to enjoy some fun with you today. Let the adult know what your plan for National Goof-Off Day will include.

You Are Invited!!
Today is National Goof-Off Day!

Come and join me in some
good-natured silliness.

Fun begins at _____.

Time: _____.

Place: _____.

We will have a few minutes of
good-natured fun by:

_____

Your fun-loving friend,

_____

Bonus: Take time to follow through with your plans.

GA1480

A Near Miss

Today is sometimes called Near Miss Day because on March 23, 1989, a huge asteroid passed very close to the earth. If it had hit our planet, its impact would have left a crater as large as Washington, D.C., and destroyed everything for 100 miles (161 km) in every direction. Pretend you are a news reporter interviewing a person who witnessed an asteroid passing over his or her house. Write your questions and the answer of each witness.

Interviewer: _____

Witness: _____

_____

Interviewer: _____

Witness: _____

_____

Interviewer: _____

Witness: _____

_____

Interviewer: _____

Witness: _____

_____

Bonus: *To create a radio talk show, have a friend play the part of the witness, and tape-record your interview.*

GA1480

Magic Birthday Candles

Did you know that magician Harry Houdini was born on this date in 1874? You can celebrate Houdini's birthday by doing a magic trick for your friends. Follow the directions below to discover a magic math trick.

1. Pick a number, any number, and write it here. _____

2. Double the mystery number._____

3. Add 10 to the answer above. _____

4. Divide the answer above by 2. _____

5. Subtract the mystery number. _____

Is your answer 5?

Here is yet another way to do this magic.

1. Pick a number, any number, and write it here. _____

2. Double the mystery number. _____

3. Add the number 22 to the answer above._____

4. Divide your last answer by 2. _____

5. Subtract the mystery number. _____

Is your answer 11?

Bonus: *Do you see a pattern in step three and the answer each time? Make Houdini proud. Explain how this number trick works!*

GA1480

March 25

Pecan Day

George Washington planted pecan trees at Mount Vernon on this day in 1775. Some of those trees are still living. Celebrate the pecan today with the pecan cookie recipe below. Can you draw a line matching the correct amount to each ingredient?

Bonus: *Use the list above to make these cookies at home.*

Sift dry ingredients together.

Cut in butter until mixture resembles cornmeal.

Add eggs and vanilla and mix well.

Shape dough in 1" (2.54 cm) balls and place 2" (5.08 cm) apart on an ungreased cookie sheet.

Place a pecan half atop each cookie.

Bake at 325° F (163° C) for 12-15 minutes.

GA1480

Make Up Your Own Holiday Day

Today is a day for making up a holiday. Each year the Wellness Permission League sponsors a day for folks to make up their own holiday. So make up your own holiday today! Use the poster below to explain your holiday to the world. Name it. Tell how it is celebrated. Explain the traditions you hope to create for celebrating your made-up holiday every March 26!

Announcement!
New Holiday Declaration

Title: _____

_____

Celebrated because _____

_____

_____

Events to take place: _____

_____

_____

_____

_____

Bonus: Do something to celebrate your made-up holiday today!

GA1480

March 27

Happy Birthday, Patty Smith Hill

Happy Birthday to you.
Happy Birthday to you.
Happy Birthday, dear Patty,
Happy Birthday to you!

Did you know that the song "Happy Birthday" is the most frequently sung song in all of the world? Patty Smith Hill, the author of this song, was born on this day in 1868. Using the tune from her birthday song, write new lyrics to celebrate a special occasion.

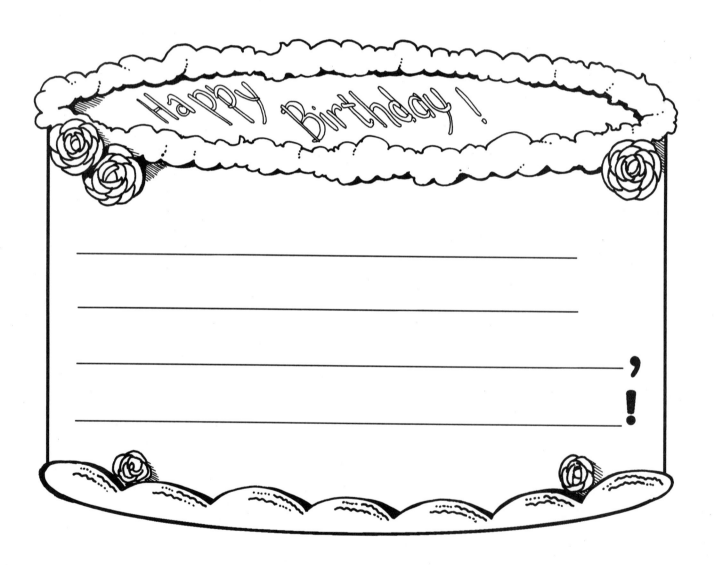

Bonus: *Sing your song to a friend.*

GA1480

March 28
Teachers' Day

Today in Czechoslovakia, children will celebrate Teachers' Day. Even though you don't live in Czechoslovakia, why not celebrate your teacher today? Think of the things that your teacher does that make you happy to come to school. List a few of them on the flowerpot below. Color or paint the flowers, cut out, and mount on construction paper. Present the bouquet of love to your teacher!

Bonus: *Pick a real spring flower tomorrow and take it to your teacher.*

GA1480

March 29

Youth Day in Taiwan

If you lived in Taiwan, today you would be celebrating your youth. If today you could celebrate being a child and do anything you wanted, what would you do all day? Use the journal below to list each activity you would cram into your day!

	8:00
	9:00
	10:00
	11:00
	Noon
	1:00
	2:00
	3:00
	4:00
	5:00
	6:00
	7:00
	8:00

Bonus: *Put stars by the things you could actually do on your next day off from school. Do them!*

GA1480

Vincent Van Gogh's Birthday

To celebrate the birthday of Vincent Van Gogh, look in an encyclopedia or art book for samples of Van Gogh's paintings. Then copy one of his paintings in the frame below. Remember, Vincent Van Gogh was especially known for his bold and powerful use of colors.

Bonus: *On the following page, design a T-shirt to represent Vincent Van Gogh and his work.*

GA1480

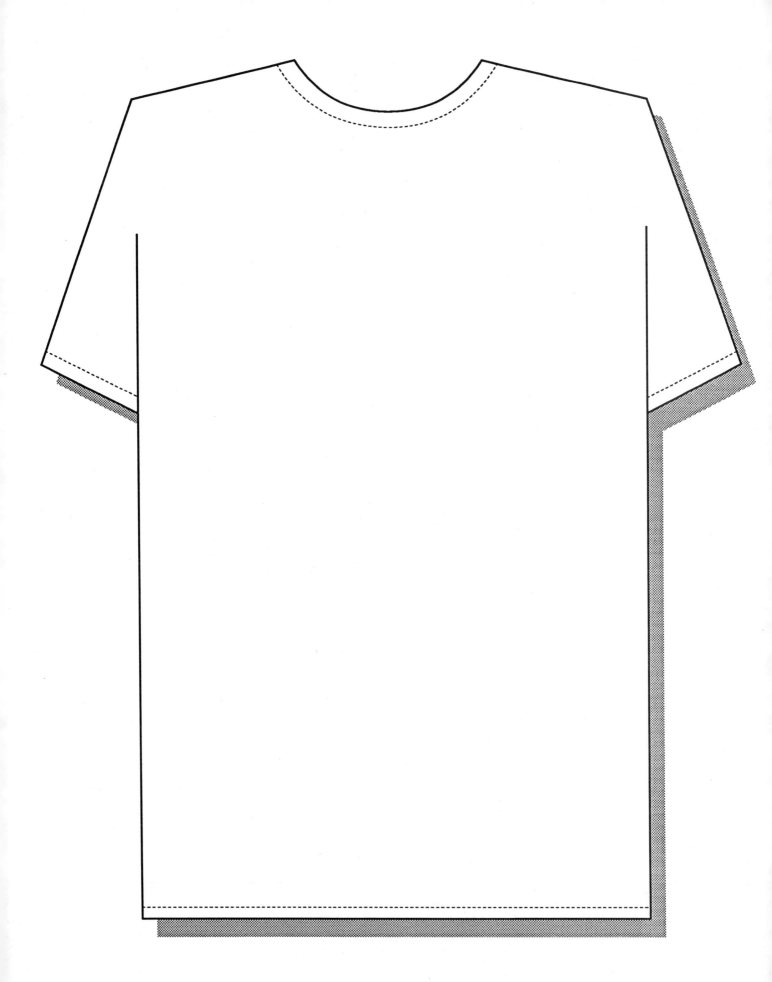

38

GA1480

March 31
A Very Big Pizza!

On March 31, 1984, Marco Cagnazzo baked a pizza that was 86 feet 7 inches (26.4 meters) in diameter. The pizza was 5895 square feet (530.5 square meters) in area. Do you wonder how many pounds of cheese were on it? Pretend you must create a pizza that will feed 1000 people. Make a grocery list of foods you will need. Don't forget to include the amount of each food item.

Bonus: *If each person ate a 6-inch (15.24-cm) square of Mr. Cagnazzo's pizza, how many people could he feed with his mammoth pie?*

GA1480

My Weather

Sunday	Monday	Tuesday	Wednesday

40

Trivia Calendar

Thursday	Friday	Saturday

41

GA1480

Use the weather stickers found below to decorate your weather calendar. Include the moon phase stickers on the appropriate dates.

42

Award Certificate
Great Trivia Historian

To: _____

For: _____

_____
Date

_____
Signature

43

GA1480

TRIVIA BONUS AWARD CERTIFICATE

TO:

FOR:

Date

Signature

44

GA1480